Why My Wife is NOT An Ass!

By Ria Pearce

ISBN 13: 978-1-885615-42-8
ISBN: 1-885615-42-6

Publisher Website:
www.vikki-lawrence.blogspot.com

Introduction

Yup, I was a wife, but since I did one of these books about husbands … well, why let us women have all the fun!

So… drawing upon extensive personal research into marriages and couple relationships, this is a ***Must-Have*** book for those considering marriage or those in a long-term relationship.

And again … you caught me. This book is full of blank pages. Even though I have looked everywhere and talked to oodles and poodles of people, I just couldn't find something good to say on the subject!

Ha.

Feel free to use this book for notes. You know, if you have any.

Enjoy!

Um… um…help?

Something good … something good … I'm still thinking….

I don’t know. You?

I give up!

I am right
Me too

I am right
Me too

I am right
Me too

I am right
Me too

I am right
Me too

I am right

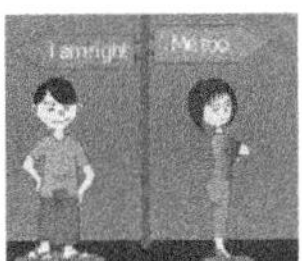
I am right
Me too

I am right
Me too

I am right
Me too

I am right
Me too

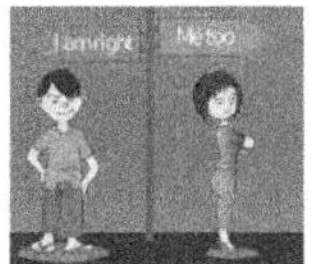
I am right
Me too

I am right
Me too

I am right
Me too

I am right
Me too

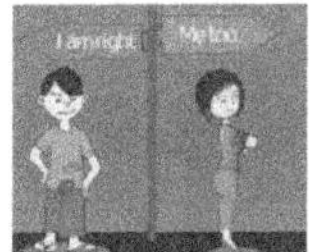
I am right
Me too

I am right
Me too

I am right
Me too

I am right
Me too

I am right
Me too

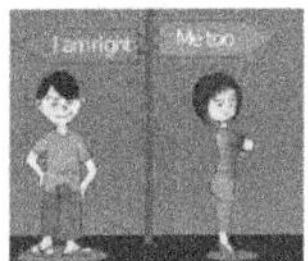
I am right
Me too

I am right
Me too

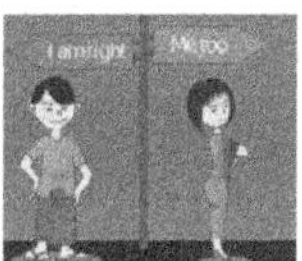

I am right
Me too

I am right.
Me too.

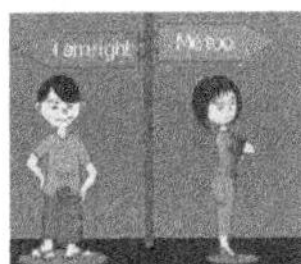
I am right
Me too

I am right
Me too

I am right
Me too

I am right
Me too

I am right
Me too

I am right
Me too

I am right
Me too

I am right
Me too

I am right

I am right
Me too

I am right
Me too

I am right
Me too

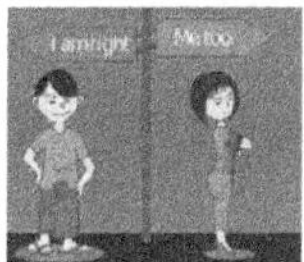
I am right
Me too

I am right
Me too

I am right
Me too

I am right
Me too

I am right

I am right
Me too

I am right
Me too

Okay … take it away!

LINKS AND CONTACT INFORMATION:

Journals/Diaries:	www.ria-pearce.blogspot.com
Survival/Prepping:	www.survival-cooking.blogspot.com
Seizures/Epilepsy:	www.seizures-suck.blogspot.com
Fiction:	www.v-lawrence.blogspot.com
Publisher's Blog:	www.vikki-lawrence.blogspot.com

www.ingramcontent.com/pod-product-compliance
Lightning Source LLC
Chambersburg PA
CBHW061032050726
47592CB00004B/1405

* 9 7 8 1 8 8 5 6 1 5 4 2 8 *